Revelation To Me

J C BEAVER

Copyright © 2012 J C BEAVER

All rights reserved.

ISBN: 10:1499783574
ISBN-13: 978-1499783575

DEDICATION

I dedicate this book to Martha and Chris.
Thank you for being my friends.
Chris, thank you for all you did to help me get this book completed
And ready to go. You are my hero!

CONTENTS

	Acknowledgments	i
1	A Door Opened	1
2	God's Door Path	5
3	Choose Servanthood	9
4	Message From Master	12
5	Esther and Ruth	16
6	Breakthrough Comes	20
7	God's Beach	23
8	Doubt and Fear	29
9	Comparisons	34
10	Understanding Blessings	41

ACKNOWLEDGMENTS

I would like to thank my husband Bill for waiting for supper many nights while I was completing this book. I would also like to thank my friend Chris for all her encouragement, help and holding my hand while I worked getting it done. To my friends who told me they were waiting for this book, thanks for waiting so long.

I would like to thank Jesus for saving me, teaching me and taking me on these adventures since day one. You are the light of my life!

1 A DOOR OPENED

After this, I looked and behold a door was opened in heaven and the first voice which I heard, as it were of a trumpet talking with me which said, "Come up hither, and I will show you things which must be hereafter, and immediately I was in the Spirit; and behold, a throne was set in heaven, and One sat on the throne, and He that sat was to look upon like a jasper and a sardine stone and a rainbow round about the throne, in sight like unto an emerald. (Rev. 1: 1-2)

What did this servant of God see? A door was opened in heaven. and the first voice which I heard as it were of a trumpet talking with me, which said, Come up (to heaven) hither (Here in this place). All these verses refer to and explain what John is talking about. I found that the bible interprets the bible and the Holy Spirit gives you understanding and wisdom. (John 10:1-2, John 10:7-9) (John 3:13) (Matthew 3:13) (Isa 58:1) (John 14:3)
We are in the last days and the Lord is shaking the earth. What will stand, will stand and what will fall, will fall. How can you stand in such a violent shaking? You must know the Lord and understand the wisdom of God so you will be able to withstand this day and come to the "come up hither." Many people believe God sends bad stuff to hit the earth, but if you know God, you know God is good. He has given you power over the elements of this world. He told us to take dominion over everything. What does taking dominion

mean? It means to have power over. It means to dominate. To govern or to permit. To bear, to have rule over. Remember the story in the Bible where Jesus was asleep in the boat. The disciples woke him up to ask Him to save them from drowning in the storm? Who stopped the storm? Well, did He start the storm so they could wake him up to stop it? No, He didn't start the storm, but He took authority over the storm and stopped it. It disturbs me to hear the news media say, when a tornado rips a town apart, "it was an act of God." No it wasn't. The act of God was keeping the people alive from what satan, the prince and power of the air, stirred up, here on earth.

I have seen many things in my life. I saw a woman on the news, praying in the Spirit, asking God to keep a tornado from hitting her home and destroying her property. She was exercising the authority God has given us to stop destruction of our homes and property. The news media said, "This is amazing, we have video footage of this woman praying as the tornado was coming directly toward her home and we see it lifting, going over her property – NOT A TREE limb is down on her property!!! She has no damage to her home at all" The news media was flabbergasted at the power of her prayer.

I have seen this happen at my home in Georgia. We live in tornado alley. When a tornado came directly through my neighborhood as I was baby-sitting the neighbor's kids, one of my neighbors came to my house terrified it was going to hit our community. I told her to sit quietly at the table, because I was praying the storm pass over, not hit or harm our homes.

She cried, "It is coming directly here according to the news. I have no shelter." The wind was picking up. It was beginning to sprinkle so I told her, "I have shelter enough for both of us and all the kids. God will not let it harm anything on this property – not even a tree limb. So hush and pray." She closed her eyes, sat at my kitchen table, holding my hands as the kids sat under the table holding hands praying. I said a simple prayer, "Abba Father, we are your children and we are in your hands, protect this property, keep an angel standing at each tree, let your Spirit watch and keep us safe."

Suddenly it began to hail and rain then stopped just as suddenly. We heard a loud roar, like a lion roaring. I opened my back door to see it had completely stopped raining. The battery-powered storm radio announced a tornado had touched down in the county before us and one had touched down in the city we lived in. We waited about two hours and left the house to ride downtown to see what had happened. We found five trees were down in town, across the road, above my house, two trees were down and the roof of the house was torn off.

God had protected us. He protects us daily. Faith means no fear in the face of the enemy. Pray without ceasing and believe God will take care of you, and HE WILL. God has given us His Holy Spirit to protect us, to teach us how to stand firm in the face of the enemy. Faith is a gift and when you exercise your faith, God will do what you believe He will do.

Now faith is the substance of things hoped for, the evidence of things not seen. (Heb. 11:1) How do you obtain a good report? By faith, we understand the worlds were framed by the word of God. This was done through faith, for without faith, it is impossible to please God. Why? If you come to God for anything, you must believe He is, and He rewards them that diligently seek Him.

Exercise is what you must do with a muscle to make it grow and make it strong. If you exercise your faith daily, God will daily make your faith strong and make it grow. He is the one who gets the work done as you ask Him to do it.

P.S. If He doesn't and you are saved you are still taken care of, or be home with the Lord. You can't lose if you believe and are saved.

2 GOD'S DOOR PATH

As I try to draw near to Father, I suddenly realized once again that today is the first day of the rest of my life. I go back to the Door remembering I got here by coming in the right Door. If I deliberately walk with Him daily. He will give me wisdom for the path He has set down for me to walk. But if I deliberately choose to go my own way, then He is not responsible for whatever mess I get myself into.

It is my choice to go to Father with questions that come to mind. It is my choice to go to Father and consult with Him on the big things and the little things that pop up in my life. It is my choice to make my own plans apart from Him. But I have to remember, when I don't consult, when I don't ask questions, when I run ahead and do it my way, then I am responsible for the outcome and can't blame Him, or anyone else, for the mess covering me in the pig-pen. Pig-pen's don't have doors, they have gates. You can see what the pigs are walloping in so it does not make sense to open the nasty gate and walk into the slop waiting inside.

The correct Door only has one knob on it. It is on your side and it is up to you to open the door and let the Saviour come in. He will not force you to get saved. You would not be happy being a slave. It is your choice to go through the Door to Father. Jesus said, I AM the door; by me if any man enter in, he shall be saved, and shall go in and out and find pasture. John 10:9 kJV

SO – Today I ran to Father and bowed before Him not only to pray, but to worship, praise, and give thanks He has written my name in the Lamb's Book of Life. He reminds me He is going to show me the beautiful path He has marked out for me. He is teaching me to be like His second Child, so I don't wonder out the Door and off the path like His first child did, and got deceived by the enemy. He says to me, "Draw near to Me my child, and read my Word. I will give you the desires of your heart as I form the image of my Son in your heart. I will set you upon the path I have marked out for you. I will keep you so I don't have to pick up the broken pieces and put you back together again. Let us walk together so you can avoid the disasters of life for I see the future. I will keep you from the enemy if you will trust and obey."

When we make up our mind to go through the correct door and not run in and out all the time, we will find the path home is lighted by the Light of the heavenly world. We won't get lost on the way home, because the Word is our direction book, it is the picture of who the Father is. When you have seen Jesus, you have seen the Father. You can't see Him without going through the correct door.

Jesus said again, Verily, verily, I say unto you, I am the door of the sheep. All that ever came before me are thieves and robbers: but the sheep did not hear them. (John 10: 7-8) God's sheep do not hear another voice. The Holy Spirit reconizes the Father and the Son. If the Holy Spirit resides in you and you reside in him, you know the truth and the truth sets you free.

3 CHOOSE SERVANTHOOD

Years ago my sister asked me, "Can you really choose whom you will serve?" I told her I would have to get back to her, I was reading the instruction book. My husband came to me recently asking me the same question. My answer to him was, "Yes Dear, you can choose everything you do daily by yes or no as I have done for the past 47 years of this marriage."

You cannot, however, serve two masters. Have you ever thought about what it means to have two masters? Let us look at this for a moment. Let us say you have a husband and a child. Have you ever thought about them being a master over your life? They are. You have to please your husband; cook, clean, go places with him, satisfy the bedroom desires. With your child, you have to take care of feeding, clothing, and many times pleasing your child. What if you had eight children and two ex-husbands?

Do you see how difficult it would become to serve more than one master?

The Bible states, no man can serve two masters; for either he will hate the one, and love the other. You cannot serve God and mammon. (Matthew 6:24 KJV) God wants to be your only Master. He has given you an instruction book to help you. He has given you the Holy Spirit to empower you and comfort you when you fail. He has given you a new heart that will desire to want to do His will. It is not hard to serve God. It is a choice. Each day we must make choices that determine our future, so it is important to make our choices yeah and amen. If America would make the the choice to say yes and no to the complicated problems that plague this nation and use the instruction book God has given us, this nation could begin a recovery that would shake the world.

And if horses and donkeys would get over themselves and become men of God, reading the instruction book and following the directions, a nation would be born again. If the President of the United States bowed his knee each morning and asked God to lead him in leading this nation, there would be a blessing upon the nation's finances and economy. It is a choice each human has to make each day. God holds nothing against a nation that repents and follows the instructions from Him.

The Bible states, *Now therefore, fear the Lord, and serve Him in sincerity and in truth, and put away the gods your fathers served on the other side of the flood and in Egypt; and serve you the Lord, and if it seems evil unto you to serve the Lord, choose you this day whom you will serve; whether the gods which your fathers served that were on the other side of the flood, or the gods of the Amorites, in whose land you dwell, but as for me and my house we will serve the Lord.*(Joshua 24: 14-15 KJV)

Most people are trying to serve two gods. This is madness. You will either hate the one and love the other for no man can serve two masters. When God says choose, He is allowing you freedom. You are not a slave. He is allowing you free choice and if you choose Him, you are still free. Let us reason together, says the Lord. (Isa 1:18)

Humans were made with a brain to choose and God gave us this brain to make decisions. Some people think they don't need God, they don't need anyone else. But have you ever been so by yourself with no one around you to talk too, no one speaking to you or you speaking to anyone? I don't believe there is a person on earth that is in that position because even in prison where one is placed in solitary confinement, someone brings food and water to them. Use your God-given brain to choose servanthood.

4 MESSAGE FROM MASTER

You and I both know when you have done wrong. The wall you build between Me and you makes Me sad and makes you discouraged. I see what is happening in your heart when you feel like no one loves or cares about you. It hurts you as badly as it hurts Me. My sadness is reflected in how you treat Me and others around you. What separates us when this happens?

You blame others for what you have done just as my children in the garden blamed the other for what they had done. Adam blamed his wife and Me, his wife blamed the serpent, the serpent stood by proudly and watched Me put My children out of the garden. Just as you pretend that I cannot understand or see what you have done, you turn and leave Me when I Am trying to help you overcome self.

I have made promises in My Word to you and if you will take the time to read it, pray, and repent, I will give to you the joy of the Lord as your strength, I will give you the peace of God to calm your thoughts, I will love you so you can experience My blessing of restoration in our relationship. Sin isn't something new to Me. I have seen it all. My Children in the garden sinned and blamed another. If they had trusted Me and took responsibility for what they had done when I asked them. I would have forgiven them and restored them to their former relationship. I would have put the serpent out of the garden. You blaming another for your sin separates US from having relationship.

I love you, Child. Remember in My Word the WORD about My child David? He was just like you only worse. He committed murder, adultery, and lied about It, I loved him through it. I did not give up on him and I will not give up on you. He didn't want to admit what he had done to start with, he didn't want to talk about it, but I continued to love him and he finally realized I was not going to give up on him. When he came to me, I loved him and restored him to a right relationship with Me, as I continued to show him how much I loved him. The wall he had built between us came down. Our relationship became even deeper than before. He didn't run from me; he ran to me.

You have not done anything, thought anything, or committed yourself to anything that I cannot forgive.

MY SON. REMEMBER MY SON.
JESUS' blood on the cross took care of all sin.

Your part is to come to Me, seek Me, talk to Me, and repent. I do so love you. Could you trust Me, just a little bit today or maybe a little more tomorrow? I love you the same all the time." *

When the Lord spoke these words to my heart, I knew it was time to quit running and settle down. I knew I needed to repent.

As the prodigal son in the pig-pen, I was getting nowhere fast, eating slop with the pigs. In my Father's house, there was food, clothing and love. I only needed to repent and go home. Would I let pride keep me in the pig-pen, or would I bow, turn, and go home? Another mouth full of slop gave me the incentive to go home. I am glad I did. Father is faithful. He loved me when I was not loveable and now He has made me into the image of his Son. Every born again Christian needs to memorize Hebrews 5:8. 'Though He were a son, yet learned He obedience by the things which He suffered'

When we go through suffering, instead of complaining and griping, we should be obedient to learn from the things we are going through. A lot of people do not learn from their mistakes, their shortcomings, or their sins. If you are going through some form of suffering right now, pray, ask God what you can learn from this. I know when I was having a hard time accepting I could never have children, I learned that God would send me children to minister too. I am a very patient person, but some mother's are not patient with their children. Many times I have been able to teach a parent, it is better to stop, count to ten, get control of your temper before you say a word. Sometimes the words said in anger, can never be taken back. Children are good at repeating what they hear their parents say.

If you have ever said more than you meant to say, you understand what I am talking about. Today might be a good day to,

Repent and come home, it is warm and safe here

5 ESTHER AND RUTH

There is a story in the Bible about a woman named Esther. She went from poor maiden to Queen of the Land. Another story about a woman named Ruth who was poor as a church mouse, but moved up in the world to become part of the lineage of the Lord Jesus Christ.

Have you ever wondered how these women made it from the street to the palace? What was it that gave these women distinction over other women going from nobody to somebody and having their names listed in the book of Books?

Let's look at Esther. The Bible states that Esther's name was Hadassah and she was brought up by Mordecai. Esther was Mordecai's uncle's daughter. She did not have a mother or father. Mordecai took Esther to be his own daughter when her parents passed away. So she was an adopted child. It says she was fair and beautiful. Esther was also a Jew. When the king of India got rid of his first wife because she would not obey and do what he told her to do, he ordered up a new Queen. To see if they were beautiful enough to be picked as Queen, the people obliged by bringing their daughters to the palace. Esther was chosen to be one of the girls who got to spend a year in the cleansing process of oils and spices for the purification of her body.

The story goes that Esther required nothing for herself except what the King desired. Whatever he liked, she would wear.

Whatever perfume he liked she wore to meet him. She was humble to the direction of others. It says she and many women went in before the King. She made an impression because he called her by name to come back to him. It states she was loved by the King and obtained grace and favor in his sight and among all of them that looked upon her.

What is there about Esther that you can relate too? What about Esther makes you angry? What is the difference in Esther and the other virgins that went before the King? If you say, "I don't know," maybe you are not looking at her closely enough. One of the things I saw in Esther was a sweet and humble heart. She was servant to the leaders in listening to their advice and following their instructions. She wanted to please the King and the people around him.

Let us look at Ruth. Ruth was the daughter-in-law of Naomi. Naomi was married to a man and had two sons. There was a famine in the land where they lived, so the husband and sons decided to leave and go to the land of Moab. While living in Moab, the son's met and married the two women that were to be Naomi's daughter-in-laws, Ophrah and Ruth. After both sons and Naomi's husband dies, Naomi decides to go home to Bethleham-Judah. The daughter, Ophrah decides to stay in the land of her birth, but Ruth wants to go with her mother-in-law, Naomi, to the land of Naomi's God.

Ruth makes a proclamation to her mother-in-law saying;

"Entreat me not to leave thee, or to return from following after thee; For whither thou goest, I will go; and where thou lodgest; I will lodge: for thy people shall be my people, and thy God my God, where thy die, I will die, and there will I be buried. The Lord do so to me, and more also, if ought but death part thee and me." (Ruth 1:16-17 KJV)

Ruth became more than a daughter-in-law to Naomi. She became her daughter. Ruth loved her like a mother and wanted only to be a help unto her. Because of her great love for Naomi, God poured out His blessing upon her and became her God. She was good and kind. She asked Naomi to let her go to the fields and glean food for the two of them. Boaz saw her and gave her grace to glean from his field more than enough to take care of herself and Naomi. Over time Boaz fell in love with her and took her to be his wife. She was in the generation that gave birth to the Christ child. Esther saved the Jewish people, Ruth was found in the linage of the Christ. God has a plan for our lives and when we make the right choices, He performs the work in our lives. God gives each person a choice to make daily. Wise people make it for the Christ of the Bible who is; The only Way, the only Truth, and the only Life.

6 BREAKTHROUGH COMES

This morning the Lord spoke to my heart and said, "You will experience a great breakthrough in your life."

Today begins a new series in my life. I have had great loss during the past years. The loss of my father, my brother, two of my Uncles, my brother-in-law, one of my husband's sisters, three of my Aunts, my nephew and my daughter. As Job exclaimed: "Shall we receive good at the hand of God and shall we not receive evil?" In all this did not Job sin with his lips? (Job 2:10)

This morning, He spoke: *"My Child, I have anointed you for breakthrough. I am the Lord, your breaker, and I will go before you. I have reconciled you to Myself through my Son and have given you the ministry of reconciliation. Your light will break forth like the morning and your healing shall spring forth speedily. You will worship Me and sing praises to My name. The end of all things is at hand, therefore breakthrough in your prayers and be ever serious and watchful for Me."*

My answer to Him: "Yes, Lord! I am willing and obedient to Your Word to me. In You, I will break through in all areas of my life. In You, I will break through in all my relationships, and in my health. I will go to new levels of praise and worship to You. I will experience a deeper prayer life, I will watch and pray according to Your will and I will prepare a place in my heart to be more serious and watchful for You to pour out Your Spirit abundantly in my life to others. Amen.

God is no respecter of person. What He does for me, He will do for you. All He requires is a broken and contrite spirit. For many are the afflictions of the righteous; but the Lord delivers him out of them all. The Lord redeemed the soul of his servants, and none of them that trust in Him shall be desolate. (Ps. 51:17)

When I got saved, I repented for the foolish things my heart desired of this world. I confessed my sin unto the Lord and He delivered me out of many trials. Over the years, I have learned that many times, God will not deliver you out of, but do you one better, deliver you through the trial, teach you a big lesson so you won't get back into that again. He will show you He is God and He is able to do what He says He will do. He gives us mighty promises and keeps them. He shows Himself Mighty God and comforts us in times of loss, or trials and sets us up to succeed. He knows the end from the beginning, and waits for us to learn.

I remember times when I was young and did not know God, He was watching over me and keeping me out of trouble. He had his hand on my life when I was born and kept me through some very troubling times. When I was a teenager and did not know anything about God, He gave His angels charge over me and took care of me, protected me and waited for the day when He would call me out of darkness into His light. The things He has taught me are life's lessons on the road to the Kingdom of God. The kingdom of heaven is in my heart, but in the Kingdom of God is where my home is being built for me, to live and worship and sing praises unto my God and my Savior for eternity.

He said to me when He saved me: "I will never leave you, nor forsake you, (Heb. 13:5) you are mine and I AM yours forever." When He makes a promise, He fulfills that promise. It might not be tomorrow, but it will be done in His time. Each time the Lord has called me to do something for Him, He always provides the way, means, money, time and shown me what it is He desires to come from it. It is so, Lord Jesus, and I confess that it may always be so.

7 GOD'S BEACH

ON THE BEACH WITH GOD –   DREAM 1
"Rest In Me" – says the Lord of Host.

I was on the beach with Jesus. We were sitting side by side. We were talking, when He took my hand and looked at the ocean where the calm water was quietly lapping at the sandy shore and the Lord said:

"Do you want to swim at your leisure, float on your back when you are too tired, hold on to the junk floating around you or do you want to be rescued and guided? When you make that final decision, whether it be today or next week, next year or down the road so far, that you have no choice but to fall out, fall down, or fall over from exhaustion. or you just give up, quit trying, I will be there to take you up. Why don't you just begin <u>now</u> to "REST IN ME"? You can rest knowing all is so safe in My hands as you allow me to guide you in everything you do. Can you rest when I tell you that rest is trust? Ceaseless activity is distrust. Without the knowledge that I AM working for you, in you, and through you, the outcome of your life will be despair and failure in the Kingdom of heaven. The Kingdom of heaven is within you, My Child. Not out there in the by and by, not at some distant place you call heaven. That is a man-made-up illusion.

Where the Holy Spirit is – is heaven. And I have declared, the Kingdom of heaven is within you. Why do you think I said, "The Kingdom of heaven sufferth violence and the violent take it by force?" (Matt 11:12) *"The Kingdom of God comes not with observation: neither shall they say, Lo here, Or, Lo there! For behold, the Kingdom of God is within You!"* (Luke 17: 20, 21) *"Verily, verily, I say unto You, except you be born again – you can not see the Kingdom of God"* (John 3:3) *The Kingdom of heaven is at hand because the Kingdom is within you. My Hand is not* *shortened that it cannot save. KNOW that, repeat it, rely on it, welcome the knowledge, delight in it for such truth is as a hope pitched out to a drowning man. With every repetition of that truth you will be pulled closer and closer to shore and to My safe haven. Let that illustration teach you a greater truth. Lay hold on it, pray it, affirm it; hold on to that TRUTH and stop activity that I do not send you to. Let go of your short- sighted activity that does not include Me. Let Me tell you what to do, when to do it and where to go to get it done. I will accomplish much through you – if you rest in Me and let Me guide you. Remember always that it is I who brought you up out of an horrible pit, out of the miry clay and set your foot upon a rock and established your goings. I AM your safety, your security and your guidance if you will only rest and obey. When a SAVED SOUL TRUST Me so entirely it seeks no more its own way but leaves all future plans to me, your Rescuer. Then will the Kingdom of God that is within you be free to exercise the Kingdom of heaven on earth. Rest equals Trust. Do you trust ME?"**

I watched the ocean water get choppier and choppier. I watched the clouds darken then draw nearer and nearer. We sat still on the beach as the storm approached closer and closer. Something inside me wanted to run off the beach. I wanted to get away from the waves that were getting higher and higher, coming closer and closer to where we sat. Lightening began to flash far off over the ocean. The sound of distant thunder as the clouds began to whirl made me tremble. I waited for Him to tell me we needed to go in. I waited for Him to tell me what to do. I waited and closed my eyes to what was coming our way. I prayed: "Into Your hands do I commit my body, soul and spirit. Into Your hands do I commit my mind, will and emotions. Into Your hands do I commit my life, my way and my truth. I waited. When I opened my eyes the clouds were white, the rain never came, the lightening stopped. There was no sound of thunder and the ocean was calm. I looked over at Jesus and He was asleep. Peace was upon His face. I held His hand tighter. I felt Him squeeze my fingers. I knew I was safe in His hand. Every day, I plan to stay at the beach with Jesus. For He is my provider, my high tower, my refuge and my strength. He has given me power over the storms of life because I commit all my life into His hands each morning and each night. I trust Him.

What did I learn from this dream? I learned that storms do not disturb God's peace. They should not disturb mine. God wants me to trust Him with everything. I made up my mind, I will trust Him. I learned that trust is leaning on, relying on and resting in His ability to get me through the storm. I learned, when it looks bad all around me, He is still in control.

Dream 2

I was sitting in a beautiful house on a piece of land that was lush with trees, green grass and a mote of water surrounding it all the way around. Across the mote was an expanse of land with trees and grass. Far in the distance was a mountain range that was grown up in dry trees. The house I was sitting in was beautiful with white carpet, a white sofa and chairs. The curtains hanging down beside the picture window were white sheers shining like the sun. I was so happy sitting in the cool of the day on the most comfortable sofa I had ever sat on.

I looked out the picture window and saw a huge ball of fire over the top of the mountain. It looked like a fireball from hell. It fell on the mountain and the mountain began to blaze and the huge fireball began to roll toward the house like lava from a volcano. I jumped up, ran to the window saying, "Oh, no, the fire is rolling toward this house. It will burn up the house. It will burn me up. I need to leave the house and find safety. I know what I will do. I will get in the water in the mote. The water will put the fire out and I will be safe." I had made up my mind how to save myself and was walking toward the door when I heard a still small voice say, "Go sit down." I stood still. Again, the voice spoke, "Go sit down, I will protect you." I did not know where the voice was coming from, but I decided the voice was what I should listen to. I went and sat down on the sofa. I watched the fireball coming across the meadow burning everything in its path.

I sat still. I watched the fireball roll into the mote. The water begin to boil rapidly. I realized if I had been in the mote, I would have been boiled to death. I heard the still small Voice say to me, "Always listen to My instructions and you will be safe. I will never harm you. I love you and will watch over you. I will protect you.

This is not your home, this is My station to train you and in My station you will learn of Me. You will come to know all about Me. You will know what I know, for in My training station you will be given the Mind of Christ and learn how to exercise My will for you daily. At the end of your time, I will take you to your home. You will know as I AM known. You are called but few are chosen. Because you obeyed my instruction, you are now chosen to learn the deep things that are hidden from the masses. My heart is yours and your heart is Mine. I will build My temple in you."

What did I learn from this dream? I learned to listen to the still small Voice of God, to be still and know He is God and no harm will come to me if I am in His care. I learned that the firey trials outside may come, but God can put them out as He keeps me safe in His care. In Him I am safe.

Dream 3

I was walking benieth the trees when suddenly I turned into a butterfly. I flew high into the sky. I looked down. There were people all around. I watched as people fought one another, killed, beat, hurt, robbed and stole from one another. Suddenly a huge light appeared in the sky and the earth became a wasteland, the people had died as the light shown on them. I looked all around. I saw no people anywhere. But there in the trees all around me, were Butterflies of all colors, all sizes and shapes. The Light was filling the whole earth with color as the wind was blowing away the ash of the dead left on the earth. He is coming.

What did I learn from this dream? I learned I can come out of the caterpillar stages of my life of crawling around in the dirt, or on the leaves of passing days and become a beautiful Butterfly. The

Light of the Lord can either change me or destroy me. I can see the wasteland, the destruction and ashes of death, hell and the grave. In the Lord, the ash is left on the ground below me. The enemy is under my feet. I can do all things through Christ Jesus, my Saviour. I learned up is better than down, those who fly with Jesus are never disappointed. I learned in HIM there are no ashes only the colorful life of the Spirit.

8 DOUBT AND FEAR

Doubt and fear are the spirits of demons who are there to stop your God given ability to faith it. They put fear in your heart and mind. Doubt and fear will stop the most aggressive work you want to do. Doubt makes you wonder if and fear makes you stop.

My advice is never doubt and have no fear! Easy to say, hard to do. So I have come up with a formula that helps me to 'stop' doubt 'if' fear arises in my heart. I watch for the faintest tremor of fear and immediately stop all work, everything I am doing comes to a stop. I get into the Word. I rest in the Lord until I know without a doubt that fear is stopped. You can deal with tired feelings the same way. Weariness will cause you to fear, cause you to get angry, cause you to be double minded.

You can rest in the Lord by finding your place to pray and read the Word. Times of withdrawal for rest always preceed fresh miracle-workings. When you learn of God, when you learn to accept the limitations of human flesh, and become obedient to the Lord, be listening too, allow Him to correct the wrong, change the unlovely, remove the junk from your junk room, you will become a new creation. He has the ability to do what you want done but can't do on your own.

The Bible says Father desires you and Jesus to become One. Think, for a moment, what that would mean to you. Everything Jesus could, can, and will do, can be done by you through Him. Everything you can't do, can get done by Him because you are subject to the law of God. Which law? The law of God is, the Ten Commandments or the abilities of the Lord Jesus Christ. In Christ, you are able to do what He desires of you because He is the One who actually does it through you. You are the temple He lives in. He has access to all things in you. You now have the mind of Christ and have access to all things in Him. How can you lose? You can't lose, if you follow the instruction book. Allow the Holy Spirit to guide you and stop running the red lights in life.

Do not seek to work for God. Never make opportunities to do work. Live in Jesus and let Jesus live in you. He will do the work and make the opportunities. The miracles will take place because He knows what is best in every circumstance. Many times people try to make things, make miracles happen. People can't make anything happen, but God who works through people can, therefore you can do all things through Christ which strengthens you. (Ph 4:13)

It is your choice to rest. It is your choice to be an example of Jesus by placing your head on the pillow of Christ's Anointing and stay asleep in the boat. When the storm rises, you have the power to stand, rebuke the storm and stop it. Do not seek to work for God, but work with God. He will lead you and direct you. He will confirm what He wants you to do, and He will do it through you

The Bible says to fear not. So why not try that for a season and see if your life changes for the better. You already know you can't make miracles happen. You already know everything you put your hands to has to have some kind of help to get it finished eventually.

What has worry been doing for you lately? Worry in my life has never done anything except give me gray hairs and wrinkles. When I stopped the worry-wart in my life, and it was a wart, (it aggravated me to death most days) the wrinkles across my brow began to fade away. The lines began to smooth out. A lady I had not seen in five years came to visit me recently and said to me, "You look ten years younger today than when I last saw you." I smiled and told her, "Ain't God good, that makes me younger than you!"

God's Word gives us instructions and we need to stop striving, stop worrying and begin to put the instructions to work for us. Just do it! Like it says in John 2:5. His mother said unto the servants, "Whatsoever He says unto you, do it!" Because they obeyed the word Jesus spoke unto them, a miracle occurred.

That is pretty simple, isn't it? Maybe this would be a good day to start doing it. Cut out fear, doubt and FAITH IT. What do I mean when I say, FAITH IT? Simply drop the fear of things in your life and start believing what God says. If God says you can do all things, can you? Sure you can. Start confessing you can do it. God will give you the power to do it.

You can ovecome it, make it happen for you and for your friends.

There are many promises in the Word. Why don't we find them and put them into practice? The other day, my sister said to me, "If you practice something long enough, you can be perfect doing it, right?" I said, "Yes, that is why we have so many perfect sinners who think they are going to heaven. They have practiced saying one thing and doing another for so long, they have deceived themselves into a state of comfort. They are lukewarm, rich, increased with goods, and have need of nothing. They don't know they are wretched, miserable, poor, blind, and naked. Sin will get you into hell if you don't repent and stop practicing it.".

That is why it is necessary to know what God's word says. When you know the word, you can be obedient to it. Jesus's blood will wash away your sin because you not only believe it, you obey and you practice it. All life choices determine your future. Why is it so hard to read God's word? The enemy of your soul does not want you to know the truth because the Truth can set you free. Isn't that what you want in this life, freedom?

I know a lady who told me she had been a Christian for over thirty years. She told me she had never read the bible all the way through. She had read a chapter here, a verse there and listened to preaching all her life. She believed she was fine with the Lord. I watched her at church go around to different people and tell tails.

She tried doing that to me once, but I told her, "Father is listening and I don't think he wants to hear that again." She never tried to tell me anything else about anyone. We have choices everyday to obey or do.

9 COMPARISONS

I witnessed to a man who was so sure he was saved even though he doesn't read his Bible, because; his excuse for not reading his bible was, 'I don't understand what I am reading.' He didn't go to church because; 'I work all the time.' He didn't pray unless; 'I had a real problem and I couldn't work it out himself.' His comment was; "I know I am saved because when I was eleven years old, I joined the church. The feeling I got was so wonderful. It felt so good. I have been a member of the church since I was eleven years old. I know, and believe, that I am saved because; 'I remember the feeling.'

He is now fifty-five years old. When I asked him about his relationship with the Lord, his reply was, "I believe in God. I don't read the Bible because I don't understand it, but I believe in God." When I asked him about his relationship with other Christian's, his comment was, "I am not a people person. I don't like being around people. I don't care about them. I believe in God and that is all that matters." When I asked him about lying to others, he replied, "sometimes you have to lie to keep from hurting someone or to get what you want." He had been married four times, now divorced and looking for another woman. He likes the drama of believing he was what he said he was and didn't care if you believed him or not.

He compared himself with a woman he knew, who is living with a man she is not married to, who believes in God, goes to church, does not read her bible either, who does not like people period. She has no friends, only the man she lives with matters to her. When he called her name and compared himself to her, I just listened quietly and thought, 'comparing yourself to other people is not God's idea of comparison for life, living, and pursuit of happiness. There is only One who God wants you to compare yourself too and His name is Jesus.' I asked him if he knew the Holy Spirit and he said, "No, who is he?" I told him he needed to ask God to introduce him to Jesus and the Holy Spirit. He didn't feel that was necessary. He believed in God.

God has a word for His people.

"Walking with Me is not a complex endeavor, my Child. Many people claim that I make too many rules, or that I require too much of them. But what do I require of My children? I made it clear through My prophets. I desire that My people act justly toward others, being fair, honest, filled with integrity. That they love mercy and pass it along to everyone they meet. And that they simply walk with Me, in humility and thankfulness for all I have done. When Jesus came, he said it another way: He told His listeners to love Me with all their heart, soul, mind and strength, and to love their neighbors as themselves. Different words, same message. Love Me, Love others, not *complicated at all."*

Father God does not require anything of unbelievers except, they REPENT, agree with His Word about His Son Jesus who died on the cross for sin. He shed blood that you can have eternal life. You ask Father to allow Jesus to come into your heart to make your life pleasing to the Father. Simple, yet to the point. Hard? No! Repenting is believing God and agreeing that you are a sinner in need of a saviour and simply asking Him for One. He already did everything necessary for you to get saved. Repent, Ask, Believe. What more do you think you need to do? He has done it all for you. "It is finished." (John19:30)

Recently, someone wanted to know why it was so difficult to know and follow God. I asked them what they thought was so difficult about following God and their answer was, "God makes so many rules. You have to give up so many things, you can't have any more fun like you once had." I asked for an example. "I can't drink, smoke, cuss, and run around with women."

I laughed as I said, "I drink all I want too, smoke whatever I want too, cuss when I want too and run around all I want too. The difference in me and you is that now I know Jesus. I don't want to do all that stuff anymore. I have a much better drink of new wine, He is called the Holy Spirit. I am so in love with Jesus that my body heats up and makes its own smoke. Cussing has been replaced with praising the Lord and shouting to the housetops. I run around with Jesus all the time now. I am happier than I have ever been running around with anyone else. When you get intimate with the Lord, you learn things that will set you to dancing. You learn secrets about life you never knew before and the joy of the Lord becomes your strength. Life is wonderful and gets better every day.

Most people today are so far away from the Lord they don't know what they are missing. Being in His presence is different from anything you might imagine. Hearing Him speak to you and tell you "well done" there is nothing like it. Many people think if they go to church and show up for two of the three services most churches offer they have done their duty.

Having a relationship with Jesus is not a duty. It is an intimate relationship where He talks, you listen. You talk, He listens. You become One with Him. It is about taking the time to get to know Him. He wrote you love letters, and we call it a Bible. You should read it sometime. He can be found at home every day, all day long, and night as well. He wants to leave the page and get involved in your life by living in your heart. It is amazing what happens when you really know Him. Think of your brain as a computer. How do you program a computer? You put the information in and when it comes out, you have accomplished many good things.

Let me tell you a little story that actually happened to me when I first got saved. My husband did not go to church with me. He was actually mad that I got saved. Why was he mad? Because I changed from his X-rated wife to a triple A wife. The night I got saved, I stopped cussing. I didn't have to try to stop. I just didn't have the words in my mouth any longer. I never took a drink again, because I didn't want it. I had no desire for alcohol from the moment I got saved. I had never gone to church, had no desire to go, but the moment I got saved, I wanted to go to church. I had never read a Bible, but the moment I got saved, I wanted to read the word and find out all I could about Jesus. I was a changed person, not because I had to give up anything, it was because I had no desire for any of the things we had been doing. We were x-rated movie goers. I had no desire to go to the movies again. One evening he decides he wants to go see an x-rated movie showing near our home. I said, "No thanks. I don't want to go. That isn't my cup of tea anymore." He got mad, turned around at me and growled, "What about what that bible of yours says about obeying your husband and submitting to him?" I stood looking at him thinking, 'here we are at a cross-road and I need Father's help answering this one.' I said, "I will have to pray about that. Excuse me for a minute." I went into the bathroom, and I prayed, "Father, I don't know how to answer him. What do you want me to do?" I heard the voice of the Lord say, "Tell him you will go with him. I will handle the rest." I went back into the living room and said, "Father said to tell you I can go." Before I could say another word, he laughed and said, "What are you going to tell your christian friends if they see you going into an x-rated movie?" I smiled as I said, "Nothing, they will be doing the same thing I am doing, obeying God." I fixed supper, we ate. As soon as supper was over, he said, "Ok, now get in the truck." I got my pocket book and went got in the truck. He lit a cigarette, got in the truck and drove to the movie theatre. It was about fifteen minutes before the movie started so we sat in the truck. He said, "Why are you doing this?" I said, "Because Father told me too." He lit another cigarette as he said, "You really going to do this?" I didn't answer. He got out of the truck, came around to open my door for me. As I stepped out of the truck, he threw his cigarette away. I smiled at him, kissed him on the lips and said quietly, "Father said, 'You are responsible before Him for anything you ask me, make me, or force me to do that is against His will.' You will have to answer before Him, not me, because you are my husband and I am in obedience." I didn't think that up, Father put that in my mind as I got out of the truck. My beloved husband smiled at me as he said, "Get your butt in the truck. I will take you to get ice cream." I got in, he shut the door and we went to the Dairy Queen for ice cream. We never went to another x-rated movie. Hearing with the ear what the Spirit speaks, works. My desire was to know Jesus and everything I could find out about Him. I also wanted to know what the Kingdom was all about. I began to study, read, and check out churches. I read the American Standard Bible from cover to cover, then purchased a King James Bible, read it from cover to cover. Then I found a Children's Word Bible and read it from cover to cover, then an Amplified Bible, read it from cover to cover. Then I found a Matthew Henry Commentary sat down and read it.

You know what I learned. There is a Holy Spirit that will teach you, speak to you, if you are willing to study to show yourself approved unto God. The Lord revealed things to me that preachers did not know. When I told one what the Lord had revealed to me, he almost had a stroke. But seven years later, he found me, apologized to me, telling me it took him five years of heavy study to find out what was revealed to me in just a few months. I told him I had been praying God would make him hungry to learn the truth, and show him, the Word is true from cover to cover. People can't dictate what God's Word says and does not say. Only the Holy Spirit is the teacher, not man, not seminaries, and not opinions. He agreed as he told me God is faithful in all that He does.

10 UNDERSTANDING REVELATION

This morning as I read Galatians 5:1-26, a still small voice began to emerge from my innermost being speaking words of love and encouragement to me. I will share this still small Voice with you, and let you experience the peace and understanding He gave me.

"You shall forever always love me with all your heart as I have spoken in My Word; You shall love me with all your mind, will and emotions; You shall love me with all your strength, for my joy is your strength. As I bestow my Spirit upon and in you, I know you will cast down all high things and arguments from man that are brought against you in judgment pertaining to My Knowledge. Any argument put forth to you by mankind as to what I have spoken, and am speaking to you, you shall bring every thought into captivity to the obedience of My Ways. Do not argue with the enemy. Stand fast in all that I speak to you. Obedience is better than sacrifice. When you pass through the rivers, they shall not overflow you and when you walk through the fire, you shall not be burned, neither shall the flame kindle upon you, for I AM the Lord your God and I will help you to obey righteousness and disallow unrighteousness. You will obey My Truths with wisdom and understanding. Then will I keep My indignation and wrath far, far away from you. You will

receive favor from My hand. Blessing along with favor, because you choose to serve and obey My Word, My Commands, My Way, My Truth. You will also receive the blessings of My Life in you forever. No more going in and going out. You will abide IN ME forever."

As Mary said to the angel of the Lord, "May it be unto me as you have said, Lord." I also say, "May it be unto me as you have said, Lord." My understanding is with obedience and following Him. I will continue to learn how to obey and follow Him. I will continue to learn what it means for the Spirit of the Lord to live big in me, and me live big in Him. I shall become God's cheerleader making the most of each day He gives me, to His honor and glory. For in my weakness, He is my strength. I know that I know that I know, what I know is coming from Him, because I am His sheep. I know His voice.and I will not follow another all the days of my life. Amen

Did you understand that if Mary had not agreeded with the angel of the Lord and said, "May it be unto me as you have said Lord" she would have never gotten pregnant with Jesus and He would not have been born. The angel spoke a blessing to Mary and she agreed with the blessing and it was so. Mary understood she had to believe as well as receive by agreeing the blessing was hers.

Will I receive the blessing of the Lord if I am not obedient to His Word. No.

Neither will you, if you are not willing and obedient.......

Most people never have a revelation of anything. They go through life wishing, hoping, and wondering if this is all there is. I use to do the same thing. But the night the angel of the Lord met with me and told me the revelation of what it means to be in relationship with the Lord Jesus Christ, my life changed. Everything in my life changed. My heart changed. My mind changed. It did not take weeks to change. That night, I changed and became a new creation.

The one thing that stuck with me all these years that rings in my heart daily is: Religion will kill you, but a relationship with the Lord Jesus Christ will give you eternal life. The other thing that stuck in my heart was, you can't have a relationship unless you get to know the person intimately. You can't get to know someone if you don't take the time to read their love letters to you.

The Bible is God's love letters to you. He spares nothing. He tells it all, the good, the bad, and the ugly. He gives insight into the details of what happened in heaven before He created the heaven and the earth. He tells you about the garden in the Bible, but He gives you details in the Spirit. Yes, the Holy Spirit will fill in the blanks and teach you the deep meaning of the hidden things of God, if you are willing to take the time to get intimate with Jesus. How do you get intimate with Jesus? Read the Word, study the Word, pray. Ask the Holy Spirit to teach you who Jesus is, what Jesus is doing, and what the Father wants to do in your heart. After the Holy Spirit shows you, it is your choice to obey the Word. It is up to you to choose to become what He has said you are, and do whatever He tells you to do. But remember, He will never tell you to do anything that cannot be backed up in His Word. The reason He wrote the book, the Bible, is so we aren't left in the dark looking for the light. He has written down all the instructions to get you to your destination. He gave Jesus to die for your sin, so you don't have to. All you have to do is believe what Father said about His only Son. What did He say? Father said, "I gave my Son because I love you so much. If you believe that My Son died in your place, you will not have to perish, you can have everlasting life." It is by faith you believe, it is by faith you receive, it is by faith you walk the daily walk. You don't have to do anything except believe and repent and receive. God will give the instruction. You obey!

Have you received a Revelation today? If not, try this one.

Do you know where the Holy Spirit Hiding Place is?

It is in two letters: M E

I say, GO GET REVELATED!

This is not a story book. This is the adventures I have had over the past 40 years with the Lord. If you haven't been on any adventures with Jesus, it is past time to start. God loves you and He will take you on the adventures of your life if you will stop looking at the future and look to what He is doing right now in your life and see it through the eyes of the Lord. He came to give you life and give it to you abundantly! (John 10:10)

ABOUT THE AUTHOR

I got saved in December 72. I was not looking for the Lord. He found me in a drycleaners, working as a customer service clerk, five days a week from 3 to 11 p.m. I was not churched as a child, so I didn't have to be reprogramed by the Father. I learned straight from the Bible with my teacher, the Holy Spirit. I read four different Bibles from Gensis to Revelations in the space of two years along with the Mathew Henry Commentary from cover to cover, straight through. I thought everybody read from cover to cover. When I had a question, I asked in prayer, "Father, allow the Holy Spirit to teach me your will and understanding of this Word. Let no corrrupt communication or deception come into teaching me. Give me the Spirit of wisdom and understanding from the Mind of Christ."

When I messed up, He cleaned me up. When I got on the wrong track by walking with wrong friends, He shook me loose and brought me home, washed me in the water of His Word as I repented, and cleaned His Child up, setting me on the right narrow road to heaven.

From day one my life changed. He is always with me, talking to me, teaching me. Keeping me close to His heart. Teaching me from His Word. Growing me up to what I am today. I give Him all the glory, honor, and praise. May God bless you!

You can contact the author by email via:

jcb2bles@yahoo.com

Books by this author:
Journey Home   Revelation To Me
Brady
David

Note:

- All scripture is from King James Version
- Word from the Lord came to me as I sat praying and meditating on Jesus
- Dreams come to me at night. Dreams from the Lord I don't forget ever.
- I pray you enjoy life here and hereafter.
- Write a journal, keep notes of what God is doing in your life, answers to prayers, and things people say to you. You will learn a lot when you reread it years later.
- May God bless and keep you, till we meet again.
- Heaven Calling 2010

J C BEAVER